I Am Unstoppable!

I AM! I CAN! I WILL!

A BOOK OF SELF-INSPIRATION
FOR CHILDREN

by

Charmaine Marie

I can do all things through Christ
who strengthens me!
Philippians 4:13

Dedication

This book is dedicated to my amazing children, Tierre, Tyeisha, and Malaika. Thank you so much for your sincere and genuine love and support. I appreciate you guys always being here for me ten toes down, no matter what. The bond we have is unmatched and I could not have asked for better children. I claim for us all, fulfilled dreams, a lifetime of happiness, and continued success.

I love you!

Mom

Thank you for taking time out to read "I Am Unstoppable". We hope you enjoy the book.

Please do a book review on Amazon.com to let us know what you think.

Published by: Real L.O.V.E. Publications
www.projectreallove.org

Cover Design and Illustrations By:
Chanel Smith & WPD Media

Cover and inside of book models:
Imery Lewis & Xayden Dunson

I Am Unstoppable!

This children's book is a work of nonfiction. Descriptions, entities, and incidents included in the story are exclusively products of the author's imagination. Any resemblance to events, and entities is entirely coincidental.

ISBN#: 9781734255140

Printed in the United States of America

I Am Unstoppable!

U - unique

N - noble

S - serene

T - talented

O - optimistic

P - prosperous

P - pristine

A - amazing

B - brilliant

L - leader

E – extraordinary

I am Unstoppable because:

I am Unique –
different, an individual, special.

My uniqueness is distinctive to me, and I am a copy of no one. I am uncommon, and my qualities are appealing in every way.

I am Unstoppable because:

I am Noble – honorable, moral, ethical.

Everything I do, I do it with the highest standards. Doing my best always, constantly delivering excellence is a way of life for me.

 I am Unstoppable because:

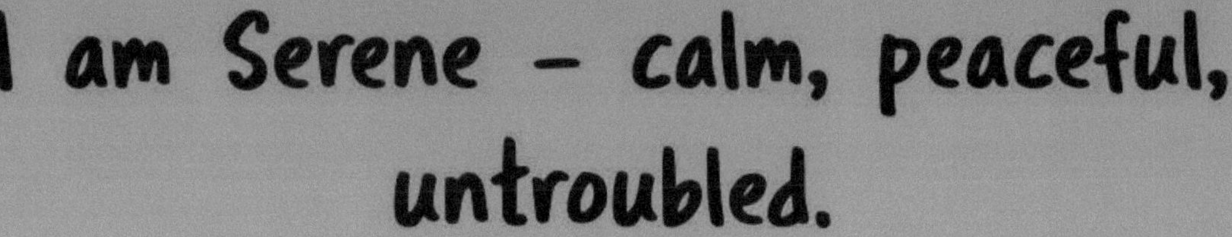

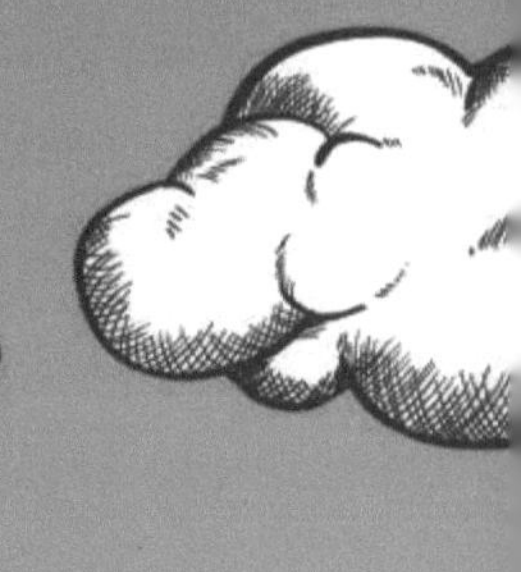

I am Serene – calm, peaceful, untroubled.

I bring the sunshine to brighten up cloudy days. I deliver a breath of fresh air and positive vibes, every time I open my mouth.

T

I am Unstoppable because:

I am Talented –
gifted, skillful, proficient.

No one else can do what I do like I do. I have got that on lock. My talents are unmatched, and my abilities are incomparable.

 I am Unstoppable because:

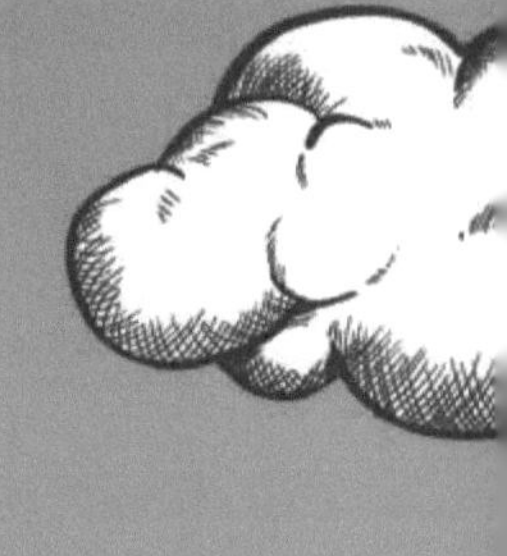

I am Optimistic – hopeful, confident, positive.

I believe in the impossible and know nothing is unreachable.
I will not stop until I see what I believe, because I know it is on the way.

I am Unstoppable because:

I am Prosperous – successful, powerful, determined.

I am thriving, growing on the inside and elevating on the outside. My strength is immeasurable, and I stand firm on what I believe.

I am Unstoppable because:

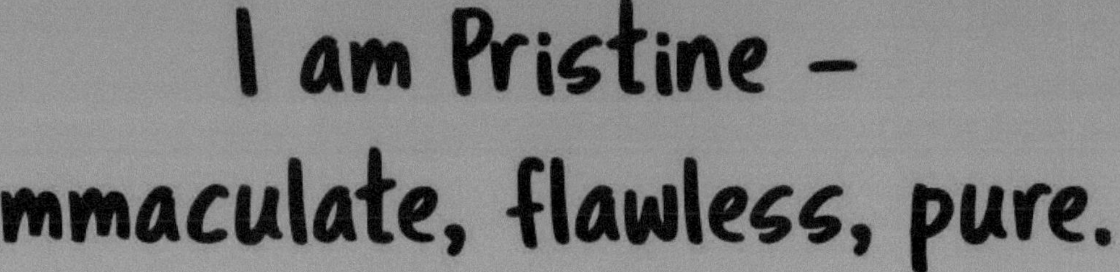

I am Pristine –
immaculate, flawless, pure.

My being is crisp, fresh, clean, and neat. Daily I re-up on perfecting me inside and out.

I am Unstoppable because:

I am Amazing –
charming, breathtaking, impressive.

Living to inspire is just what I do as I become a better me, watching what motivates my mind and stimulates my being.

 I am Unstoppable because:

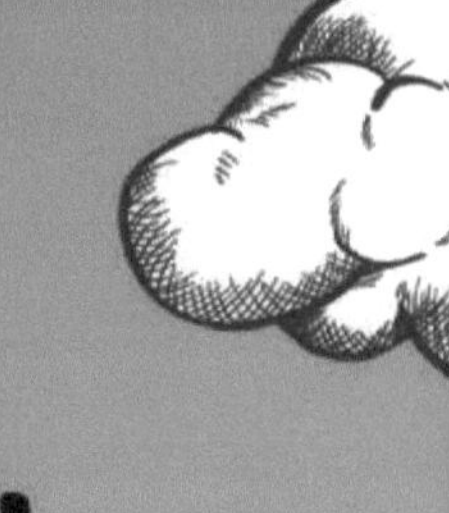

I am Brilliant -
bright, clever, intellectual.

Knowledgeable through my research and scholarly because of my studies, I become empowering down on the inside, and reveal wisdom to all I encounter.

L

I am
Unstoppable
because:

I am a Leader.

- ❖ Frontrunner
- ❖ Trailblazer
- ❖ Groundbreaker

That's Me!

I positively impact and inspire those who choose to follow in my footsteps.

E
I am
Unstoppable
because:

I am Extraordinary –
– remarkable, exceptional, sensational.

Just ordinary will not do!
Uncommon, peculiar, special, not
your norm – I am unstoppable!

I Am Unstoppable!

U - unique

N - noble

S - serene

T - talented

O - optimistic

P - prosperous

P - pristine

A - amazing

B - brilliant

L - leader

E – extraordinary

I Am Beautiful

THE BEHOLDER IS ME

COMING SOON!!!

We really appreciate you taking time out to read I Am Unstoppable. Please do a review on Amazon.com to let us know what you think. Be sure to let your family and friends know about the I Am series.

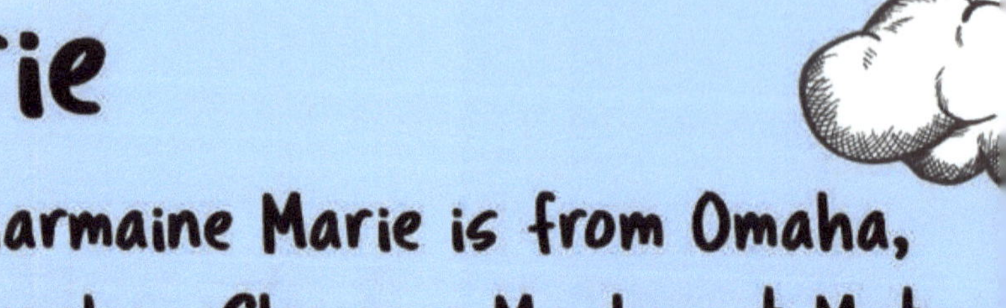

Meet
Charmaine Marie

Charmaine Marie is from Omaha, Nebraska. She is a Machinist Mate in the World's Greatest Navy, and the Chief Executive Officer of Real (L.O.V.E.) Leadership Obedience Victory and Excellence, where she administers a Life Skills Program called Success At Its Best, for youth. Additionally, Charmaine Marie is an author, screenwriter, public speaker, and poet. Her passion is helping youth to be successful in this world.